Me and My Friends

Diana Lynn

Published by D&D Graphics in 2017
First edition; First printing

Design and writing © 2017 Diana Lynn

All rights reserved. No part of this book may be reproduced or transmitted in any form or by any means, including but not limited to information storage and retrieval systems, electronic, mechanical, photocopy, recording, etc. without written permission from the copyright holder.

ISBN: 978-1-947594-91-3

Many Thanks to:

Missy Kirtley, Alice Farmer and TM Caldwell, Kat Jacobsen

The first few pages are to write about yourself. The rest of the book is to write about your friends.

Use the Table of Contents to quickly find the page your friend is listed on.

This book belongs to:

_____

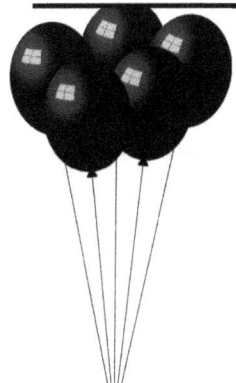

Date: _____

Grade: _____

_____
Email Address (optional)

_____
Twitter (optional)

_____
Instagram (optional)

_____
Tumblr (optional)

_____
Snapchat (optional)

_____
Phone # (optional)

Table of Contents

Friend's Name	Page #
	12
	16
	20
	24
	28
	32
	36
	40
	44
	48
	52
	56
	60
	64
	68
	72
	76
	80

Table of Contents

Friend's Name	Page #
	84
	88
	92
	96
	100
	104
	108
	112
	116
	120
	124
	128
	132
	136
	140
	144
	148
	152

Extra! Extra! Read All About Me!

My Story Told Here!

Birthday: _____   Birthstone: _____

A picture of me:

Caption:
_____
_____
_____

Favorite Apps:
_____
_____
_____
_____
_____
_____
_____
_____
_____
_____
_____
_____
_____

I Live With:
_____
_____
_____
_____
_____

When I Grow Up I Want To Be:
_____
_____
_____
_____
_____

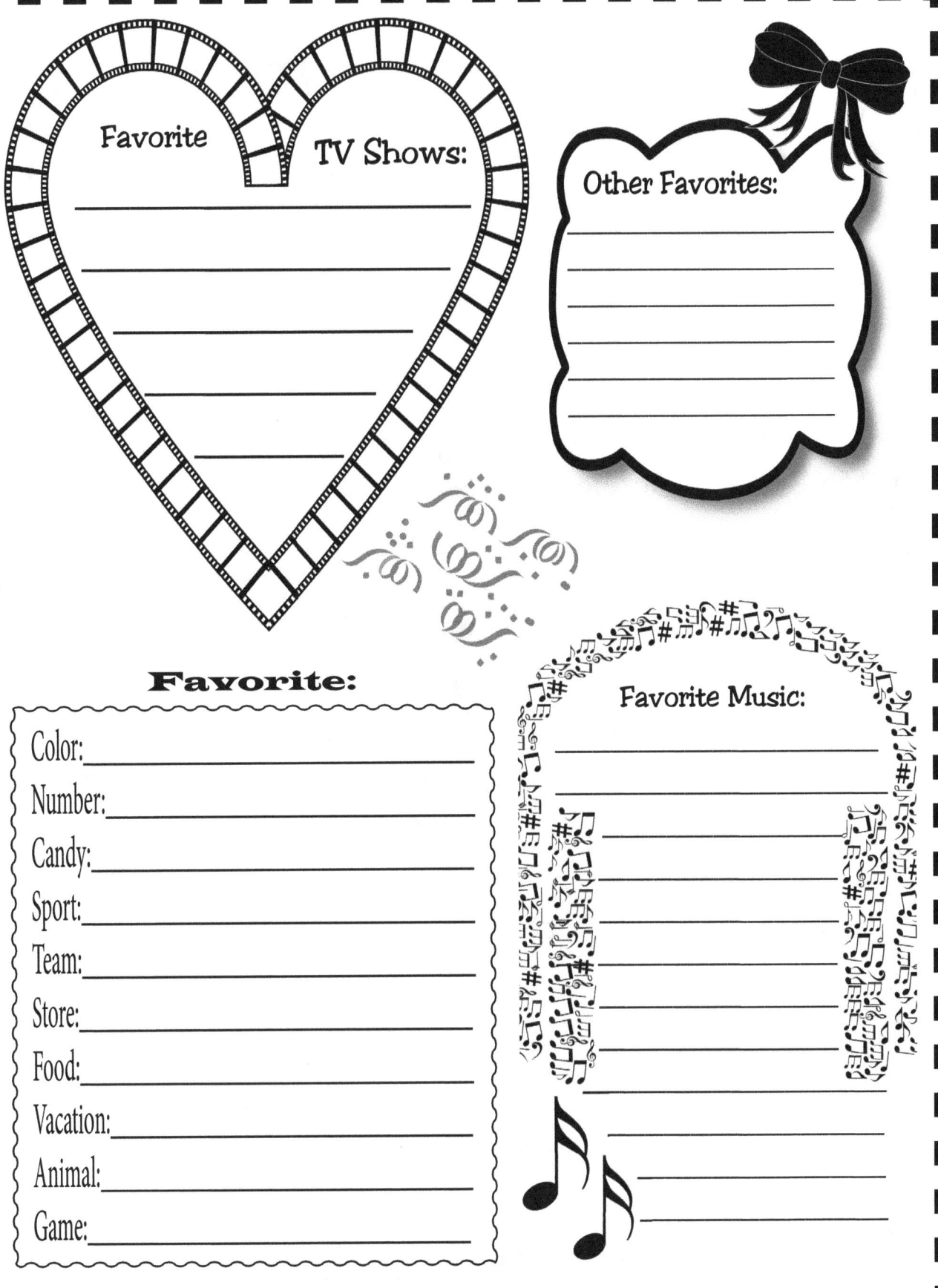

All About My Friend!

Name: _____

🧁 Birthday: _____   💎 Birthstone: _____

A Picture of My Friend:

Caption:
_____
_____
_____

Favorite Apps:
_____
_____
_____
_____
_____
_____
_____
_____
_____
_____
_____

Family:
_____
_____
_____
_____
_____

When They Grow Up They Want To Be:
_____
_____
_____
_____
_____

Favorite TV Shows:
_____
_____
_____
_____
_____

Other Favorites:
_____
_____
_____
_____
_____
_____

Favorite:

Color:_____
Number:_____
Candy:_____
Sport:_____
Team:_____
Store:_____
Food:_____
Vacation:_____
Animal:_____
Game:_____

Favorite Music:
_____
_____
_____
_____
_____
_____
_____

Hobbies: _____
_____
_____
_____

Favorite Books:
_____
_____
_____
_____

Favorite Place to Be:
_____
_____
_____
_____
_____
_____

My Friend's Wish:
_____ _____
_____ _____
_____ _____
_____ _____
_____ _____
_____ _____

Favorite Meal/Food:

Favorite Subject In School:

Collections:

Notes:

All About My Friend!

Name: _____

🧁 Birthday: _____   💎 Birthstone: _____

A Picture of My Friend:

Caption:
_____
_____
_____

Favorite Apps:
_____
_____
_____
_____
_____
_____
_____
_____
_____
_____
_____

Family:
_____
_____
_____
_____

When They Grow Up They Want To Be:
_____
_____
_____
_____

Favorite TV Shows:
_____
_____
_____
_____
_____

Other Favorites:
_____
_____
_____
_____
_____
_____

Favorite:

Color: _____
Number: _____
Candy: _____
Sport: _____
Team: _____
Store: _____
Food: _____
Vacation: _____
Animal: _____
Game: _____

Favorite Music:
_____
_____
_____
_____
_____
_____
_____

Hobbies: _____
_____
_____
_____

Favorite Books:
_____
_____
_____

Favorite Place to Be:
_____
_____
_____
_____
_____
_____

My Friend's Wish:
_____ _____
_____ _____
_____ _____
_____ _____
_____ _____

Favorite Meal/Food:

Favorite Subject In School:

Collections:

Notes:

All About My Friend!

Name: _____

🧁 **Birthday:** _____ 💎 **Birthstone:** _____

A Picture of My Friend:

Caption:
_____
_____
_____

Favorite Apps:
_____
_____
_____
_____
_____
_____
_____
_____
_____
_____
_____

Family:
_____
_____
_____
_____

When They Grow Up They Want To Be:
_____
_____
_____
_____

Favorite TV Shows:
_____
_____
_____
_____
_____

Other Favorites:
_____
_____
_____
_____
_____
_____

Favorite:

Color:_____
Number:_____
Candy:_____
Sport:_____
Team:_____
Store:_____
Food:_____
Vacation:_____
Animal:_____
Game:_____

Favorite Music:
_____
_____
_____
_____
_____

Hobbies: _____
_____
_____
_____

Favorite Books:
_____
_____
_____
_____

Favorite Place to Be:
_____
_____
_____
_____
_____
_____

My Friend's Wish:
_____
_____
_____
_____
_____

Favorite Meal/Food:

Favorite Subject In School:

Collections:

Notes:

All About My Friend!

Name: _____

🧁 **Birthday:** _____   💎 **Birthstone:** _____

A Picture of My Friend:

Caption: _____

Favorite Apps:
_____

Family:
_____

When They Grow Up They Want To Be:
_____

Page 24

Favorite TV Shows:
_____
_____
_____
_____

Other Favorites:
_____
_____
_____
_____
_____
_____

Favorite:
Color:_____
Number:_____
Candy:_____
Sport:_____
Team:_____
Store:_____
Food:_____
Vacation:_____
Animal:_____
Game:_____

Favorite Music:
_____
_____
_____
_____
_____
_____

Hobbies: _____
_____
_____
_____

Favorite Books:
_____
_____
_____
_____

Favorite Place to Be:
_____
_____
_____
_____
_____
_____
_____

My Friend's Wish:
_____ _____
_____ _____
_____ _____
_____ _____
_____ _____

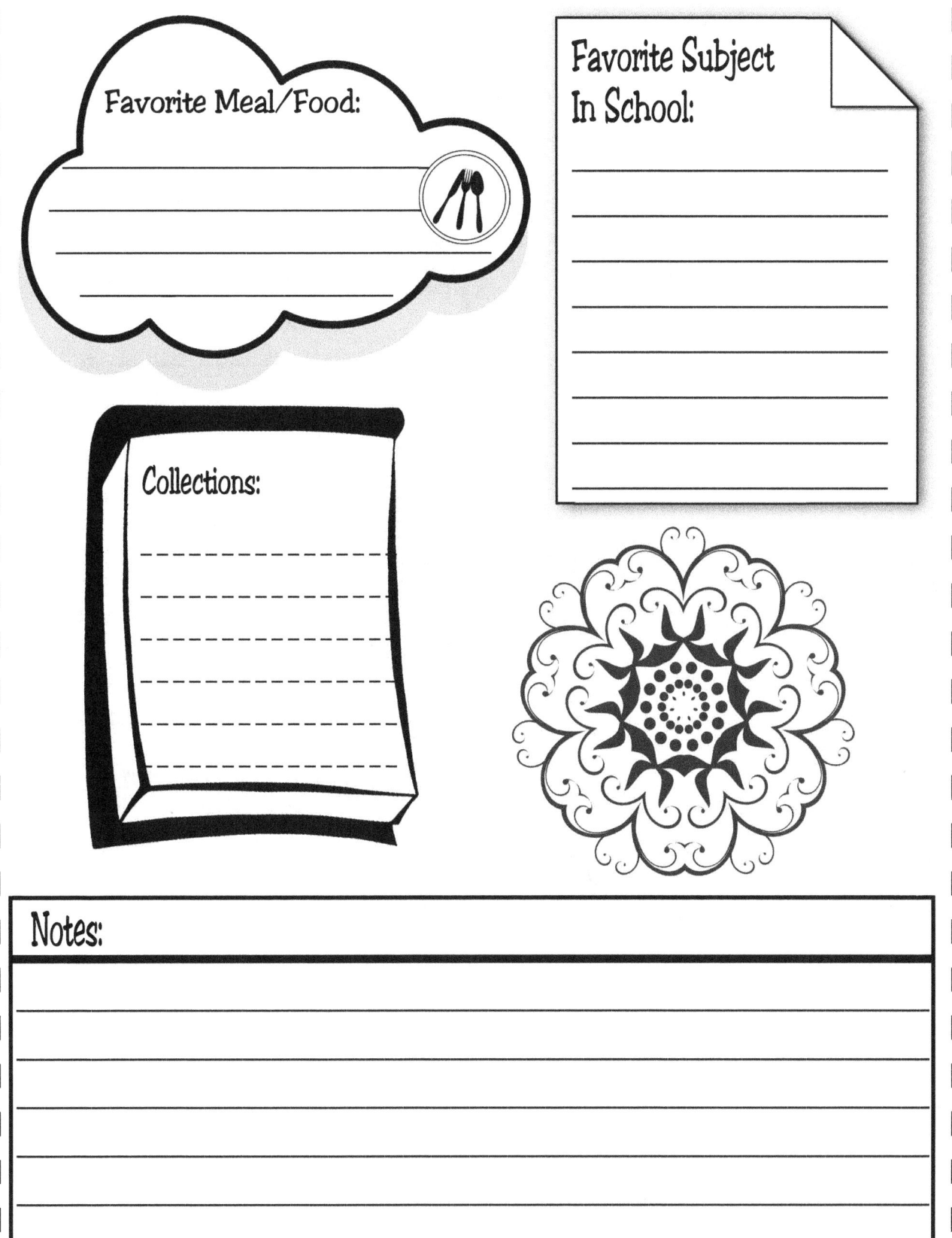

All About My Friend!

Name: _____

🧁 Birthday: _____   💎 Birthstone: _____

A Picture of My Friend:

Caption:
_____
_____
_____

Favorite Apps:
_____
_____
_____
_____
_____
_____
_____
_____
_____
_____
_____

Family:
_____
_____
_____
_____

When They Grow Up They Want To Be:
_____
_____
_____
_____

Favorite TV Shows:
_____
_____
_____
_____
_____

Other Favorites:
_____
_____
_____
_____
_____

Favorite:

Color:_____
Number:_____
Candy:_____
Sport:_____
Team:_____
Store:_____
Food:_____
Vacation:_____
Animal:_____
Game:_____

Favorite Music:
_____
_____
_____
_____
_____

Hobbies: _____
_____
_____
_____

Favorite Books:
_____
_____
_____

Favorite Place to Be:
_____
_____
_____
_____
_____

My Friend's Wish:
_____ _____
_____ _____
_____ _____
_____ _____

All About My Friend!

Name: _____

🧁 Birthday: _____ 💎 Birthstone: _____

A Picture of My Friend:

Caption:
_____
_____
_____

Favorite Apps:
_____
_____
_____
_____
_____
_____
_____
_____
_____
_____

Family:
_____
_____
_____
_____

When They Grow Up They Want To Be:
_____
_____
_____
_____

Favorite TV Shows:
_____
_____
_____
_____
_____

Other Favorites:
_____
_____
_____
_____
_____
_____

Favorite:

Color:_____
Number:_____
Candy:_____
Sport:_____
Team:_____
Store:_____
Food:_____
Vacation:_____
Animal:_____
Game:_____

Favorite Music:
_____
_____
_____
_____
_____
_____

Hobbies: _____
_____
_____
_____

Favorite Books:
_____
_____
_____
_____

Favorite Place to Be:
_____
_____
_____
_____
_____
_____

My Friend's Wish:
_____ _____
_____ _____
_____ _____
_____ _____
_____ _____

Favorite Meal/Food:
_____
_____
_____

Favorite Subject In School:
_____
_____
_____
_____
_____
_____
_____
_____

Collections:
_____
_____
_____
_____
_____
_____

Notes:
_____
_____
_____
_____
_____

All About My Friend!

Name: _____

Birthday: _____   Birthstone: _____

A Picture of My Friend:

Caption:
_____
_____
_____

Favorite Apps:
_____
_____
_____
_____
_____
_____
_____
_____
_____
_____

Family:
_____
_____
_____
_____

When They Grow Up They Want To Be:
_____
_____
_____
_____

Favorite TV Shows:
_____
_____
_____
_____
_____

Other Favorites:
_____
_____
_____
_____
_____

Favorite:

Color: _____
Number: _____
Candy: _____
Sport: _____
Team: _____
Store: _____
Food: _____
Vacation: _____
Animal: _____
Game: _____

Favorite Music:
_____
_____
_____
_____
_____

Hobbies: _____
_____
_____
_____

Favorite Books:
_____
_____
_____
_____

Favorite Place to Be:
_____
_____
_____
_____
_____
_____

My Friend's Wish:
_____ _____
_____ _____
_____ _____
_____ _____
_____ _____

All About My Friend!

Name: _____

🧁 Birthday: _____   💎 Birthstone: _____

A Picture of My Friend:

Caption:
_____
_____
_____

Favorite Apps:
_____
_____
_____
_____
_____
_____
_____
_____
_____
_____
_____
_____
_____

Family:
_____
_____
_____
_____
_____

When They Grow Up They Want To Be:
_____
_____
_____
_____
_____

Favorite TV Shows:

_____
_____
_____
_____
_____

Other Favorites:

_____
_____
_____
_____
_____

Favorite:

Color: _____
Number: _____
Candy: _____
Sport: _____
Team: _____
Store: _____
Food: _____
Vacation: _____
Animal: _____
Game: _____

Favorite Music:

_____
_____
_____
_____
_____

Hobbies: _____
_____
_____
_____

Favorite Books:
_____
_____
_____
_____

Favorite Place to Be:
_____
_____
_____
_____
_____
_____
_____

My Friend's Wish:
_____ _____
_____ _____
_____ _____
_____ _____
_____ _____
_____ _____

Page 42

Favorite Meal/Food:

Favorite Subject In School:

Collections:

Notes:

All About My Friend!

Name: _____

Birthday: _____   Birthstone: _____

A Picture of My Friend:

Caption:
_____
_____
_____

Favorite Apps:
_____
_____
_____
_____
_____
_____
_____
_____
_____
_____

Family:
_____
_____
_____
_____
_____

When They Grow Up They Want To Be:
_____
_____
_____
_____

Favorite TV Shows:
_____
_____
_____
_____

Other Favorites:
_____
_____
_____
_____
_____

Favorite:

Color: _____
Number: _____
Candy: _____
Sport: _____
Team: _____
Store: _____
Food: _____
Vacation: _____
Animal: _____
Game: _____

Favorite Music:
_____
_____
_____
_____
_____
_____
_____

Hobbies: _____
_____
_____
_____

Favorite Books:
_____
_____
_____
_____

Favorite Place to Be:
_____
_____
_____
_____
_____

My Friend's Wish:
_____   _____
_____   _____
_____   _____
_____   _____

Favorite Meal/Food:

Favorite Subject In School:

Collections:

Notes:

All About My Friend!

Name: _____

🧁 Birthday: _____   💎 Birthstone: _____

A Picture of My Friend:

Caption:
_____
_____
_____

Favorite Apps:
_____
_____
_____
_____
_____
_____
_____
_____
_____
_____
_____
_____

Family:
_____
_____
_____
_____
_____

When They Grow Up They Want To Be:
_____
_____
_____
_____
_____

Favorite TV Shows:
_____
_____
_____
_____
_____

Other Favorites:
_____
_____
_____
_____
_____

Favorite:

Color: _____
Number: _____
Candy: _____
Sport: _____
Team: _____
Store: _____
Food: _____
Vacation: _____
Animal: _____
Game: _____

Favorite Music:
_____
_____
_____
_____
_____
_____

Hobbies: _____
_____
_____
_____

Favorite Books:
_____
_____
_____
_____

Favorite Place to Be:
_____
_____
_____
_____
_____
_____

My Friend's Wish:
_____ _____
_____ _____
_____ _____
_____ _____
_____ _____

All About My Friend!

Name: _____

🧁 **Birthday:** _____ 💎 **Birthstone:** _____

A Picture of My Friend:

Caption: _____

Favorite Apps:
_____
_____
_____
_____
_____
_____
_____
_____
_____
_____
_____

Family:
_____
_____
_____
_____
_____

When They Grow Up They Want To Be:
_____
_____
_____
_____
_____

Favorite TV Shows:
_____
_____
_____
_____
_____

Other Favorites:
_____
_____
_____
_____
_____
_____

Favorite:

Color: _____
Number: _____
Candy: _____
Sport: _____
Team: _____
Store: _____
Food: _____
Vacation: _____
Animal: _____
Game: _____

Favorite Music:
_____
_____
_____
_____
_____
_____
_____
_____

Hobbies: _____
_____
_____
_____

Favorite Books:
_____
_____
_____
_____

Favorite Place to Be:
_____
_____
_____
_____
_____
_____
_____

My Friend's Wish:
_____   _____
_____   _____
_____   _____
_____   _____
_____   _____

All About My Friend!

Name: _____

🧁 Birthday: _____   💎 Birthstone: _____

A Picture of My Friend:

Caption: _____
_____
_____

Favorite Apps:
_____
_____
_____
_____
_____
_____
_____
_____
_____
_____
_____
_____

Family:
_____
_____
_____
_____

When They Grow Up They Want To Be:
_____
_____
_____
_____

Favorite TV Shows:
_____
_____
_____
_____
_____

Other Favorites:
_____
_____
_____
_____
_____
_____

Favorite:

Color:_____
Number:_____
Candy:_____
Sport:_____
Team:_____
Store:_____
Food:_____
Vacation:_____
Animal:_____
Game:_____

Favorite Music:
_____
_____
_____
_____
_____
_____

Hobbies: _____
_____
_____
_____

Favorite Books:
_____
_____
_____
_____

Favorite Place to Be:
_____
_____
_____
_____
_____
_____

My Friend's Wish:
_____ _____
_____ _____
_____ _____
_____ _____
_____ _____

Favorite Meal/Food:

Favorite Subject In School:

Collections:

Notes:

All About My Friend!

Name: _____

🧁 Birthday: _____ 💎 Birthstone: _____

A Picture of My Friend:

Caption:
_____
_____
_____

Favorite Apps:
_____
_____
_____
_____
_____
_____
_____
_____
_____
_____

Family:
_____
_____
_____
_____

When They Grow Up They Want To Be:
_____
_____
_____
_____

Favorite TV Shows:
_____
_____
_____
_____

Other Favorites:
_____
_____
_____
_____
_____
_____

Favorite:

Color:_____
Number:_____
Candy:_____
Sport:_____
Team:_____
Store:_____
Food:_____
Vacation:_____
Animal:_____
Game:_____

Favorite Music:
_____
_____
_____
_____
_____
_____

Hobbies: _____
_____
_____
_____

Favorite Books:
_____
_____
_____
_____

Favorite Place to Be:
_____
_____
_____
_____
_____

My Friend's Wish:
_____ _____
_____ _____
_____ _____
_____ _____
_____ _____

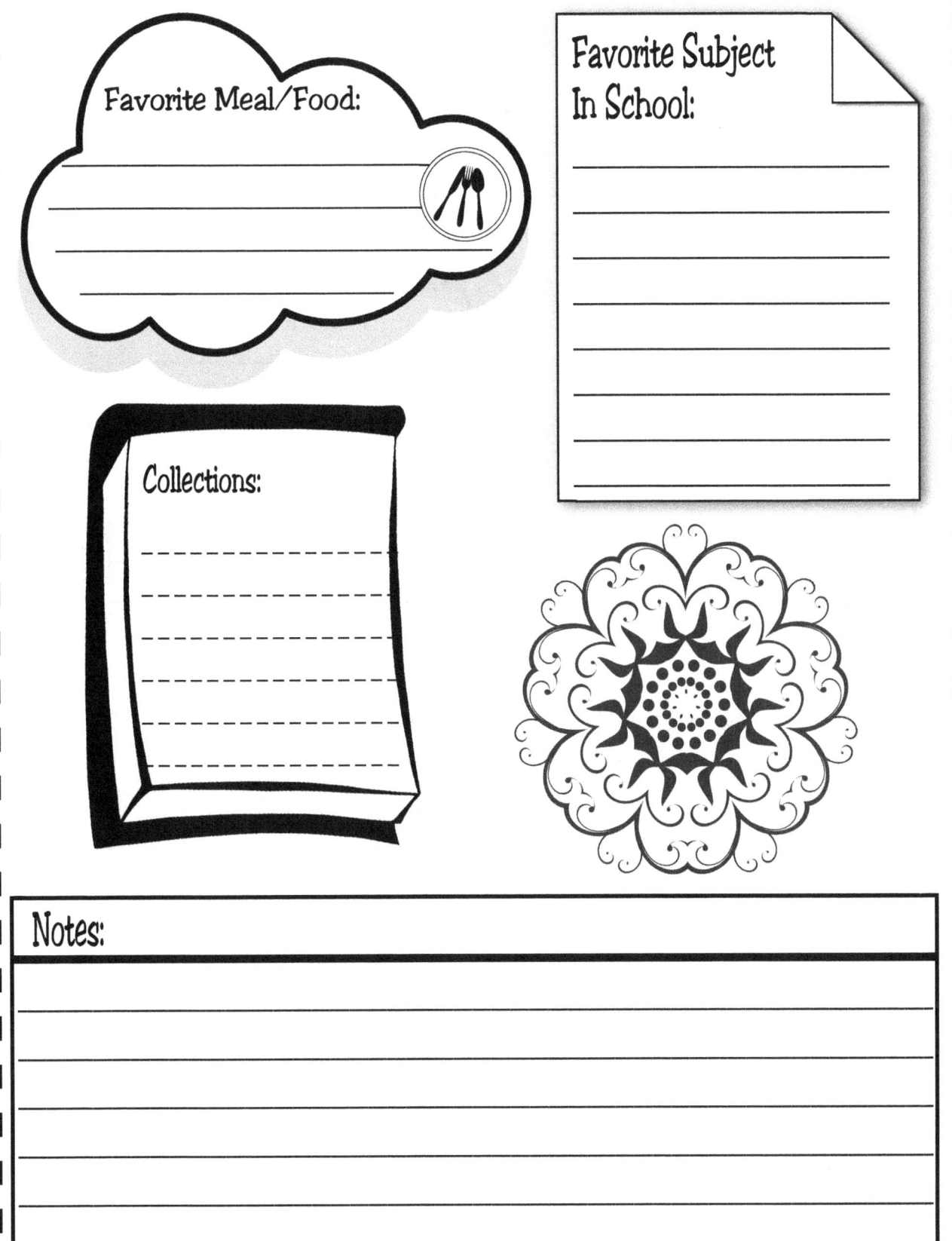

All About My Friend!

Name: _____

🧁 Birthday: _____ 💎 Birthstone: _____

A Picture of My Friend:

Caption: _____
_____
_____

Favorite Apps:
_____
_____
_____
_____
_____
_____
_____
_____
_____
_____

Family:
_____
_____
_____
_____

When They Grow Up They Want To Be:
_____
_____
_____
_____

Favorite TV Shows:
_____
_____
_____
_____

Other Favorites:
_____
_____
_____
_____
_____
_____

Favorite:

Color: _____
Number: _____
Candy: _____
Sport: _____
Team: _____
Store: _____
Food: _____
Vacation: _____
Animal: _____
Game: _____

Favorite Music:
_____
_____
_____
_____
_____
_____
_____

Hobbies: _____
_____
_____
_____

Favorite Books:
_____
_____
_____
_____

Favorite Place to Be:
_____
_____
_____
_____
_____

My Friend's Wish:
_____ _____
_____ _____
_____ _____
_____ _____

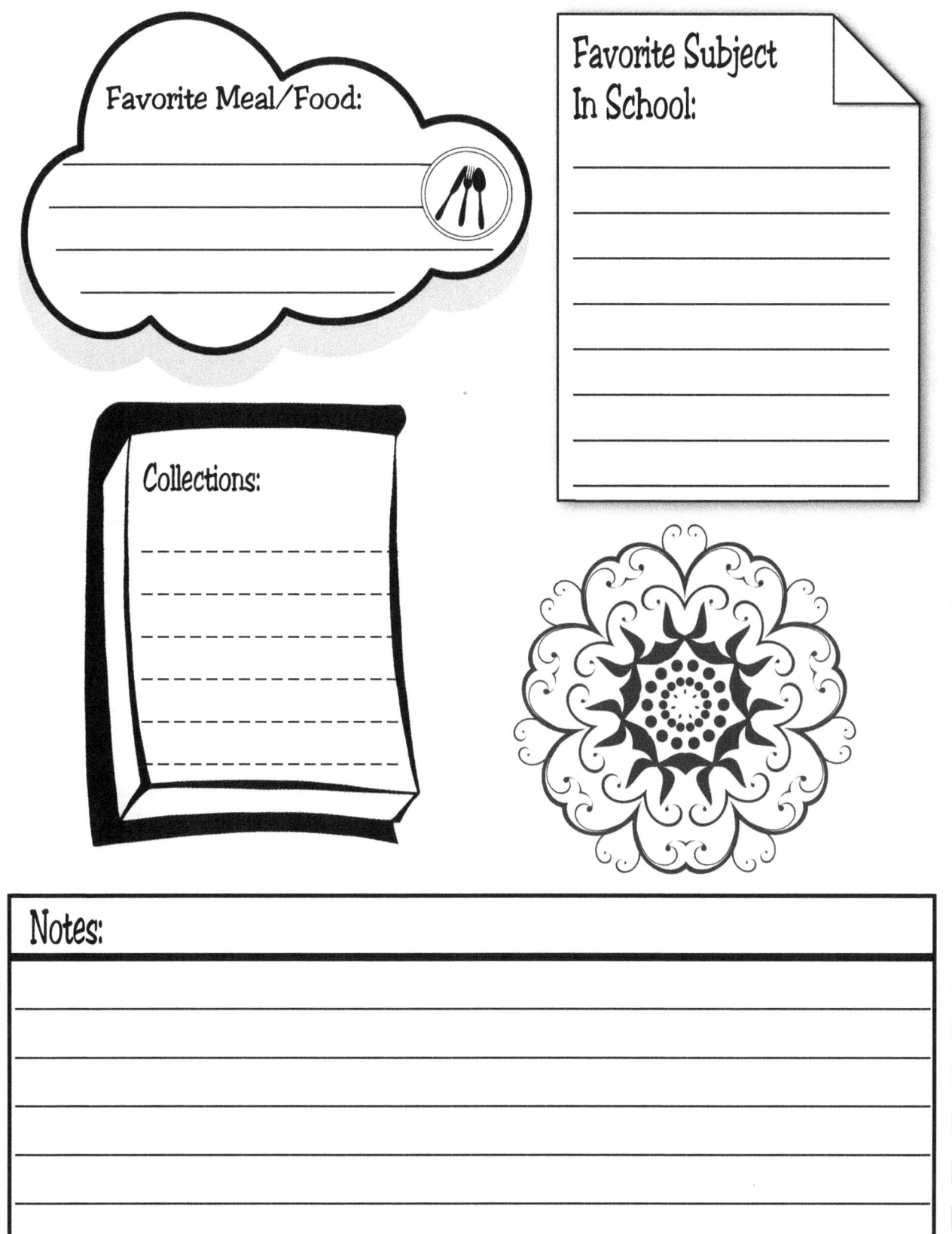

All About My Friend!

Name: _____

Birthday: _____ Birthstone: _____

A Picture of My Friend:

Caption:
_____
_____
_____

Favorite Apps:
_____
_____
_____
_____
_____
_____
_____
_____
_____
_____
_____
_____

Family:
_____
_____
_____
_____
_____

When They Grow Up They Want To Be:
_____
_____
_____
_____
_____

Favorite TV Shows:
_____
_____
_____
_____

Other Favorites:
_____
_____
_____
_____
_____
_____

Favorite:

Color:_____
Number:_____
Candy:_____
Sport:_____
Team:_____
Store:_____
Food:_____
Vacation:_____
Animal:_____
Game:_____

Favorite Music:
_____
_____
_____
_____
_____
_____

Hobbies: _____
_____
_____
_____

Favorite Books:
_____
_____
_____
_____

Favorite Place to Be:
_____
_____
_____
_____
_____
_____

My Friend's Wish:
_____   _____
_____   _____
_____   _____
_____   _____
_____   _____

All About My Friend!

_____
Name:

🧁 Birthday: _____   💎 Birthstone: _____

A Picture of My Friend:

Caption:
_____
_____
_____

Favorite Apps:
_____
_____
_____
_____
_____
_____
_____
_____
_____
_____
_____

Family:
_____
_____
_____
_____
_____

When They Grow Up They Want To Be:
_____
_____
_____
_____
_____

Favorite TV Shows:
_____
_____
_____
_____
_____

Other Favorites:
_____
_____
_____
_____
_____

Favorite:

Color: _____
Number: _____
Candy: _____
Sport: _____
Team: _____
Store: _____
Food: _____
Vacation: _____
Animal: _____
Game: _____

Favorite Music:
_____
_____
_____
_____
_____

Hobbies: _____
_____
_____
_____

Favorite Books:
_____
_____
_____
_____

Favorite Place to Be:
_____
_____
_____
_____
_____

My Friend's Wish:
_____
_____
_____
_____
_____

Favorite Meal/Food:
_____
_____
_____

Favorite Subject In School:
_____
_____
_____
_____
_____
_____
_____

Collections:
_____
_____
_____
_____
_____
_____

Notes:
_____
_____
_____
_____
_____

All About My Friend!

Name: _____

Birthday: _____   Birthstone: _____

A Picture of My Friend:

Caption:
_____
_____
_____

Favorite Apps:
_____
_____
_____
_____
_____
_____
_____
_____
_____
_____
_____
_____

Family:
_____
_____
_____
_____

When They Grow Up They Want To Be:
_____
_____
_____
_____

Favorite TV Shows:
_____
_____
_____
_____

Other Favorites:
_____
_____
_____
_____
_____

Favorite:

Color:_____
Number:_____
Candy:_____
Sport:_____
Team:_____
Store:_____
Food:_____
Vacation:_____
Animal:_____
Game:_____

Favorite Music:
_____
_____
_____
_____
_____
_____

Hobbies: _____
_____
_____
_____

Favorite Books:
_____
_____
_____

Favorite Place to Be:
_____
_____
_____
_____
_____

My Friend's Wish:
_____ _____
_____ _____
_____ _____
_____ _____

Favorite Meal/Food:

Favorite Subject In School:

Collections:

Notes:

All About My Friend!

Name: _____

🧁 Birthday: _____ 💎 Birthstone: _____

A Picture of My Friend:

Caption:
_____
_____
_____

Favorite Apps:
_____
_____
_____
_____
_____
_____
_____
_____
_____
_____
_____
_____
_____

Family:
_____
_____
_____
_____

When They Grow Up They Want To Be:
_____
_____
_____
_____

Favorite TV Shows:

_____
_____
_____
_____

Other Favorites:

_____
_____
_____
_____
_____
_____

Favorite:

Color:_____
Number:_____
Candy:_____
Sport:_____
Team:_____
Store:_____
Food:_____
Vacation:_____
Animal:_____
Game:_____

Favorite Music:

_____
_____
_____
_____
_____
_____

Hobbies: _____
_____
_____
_____

Favorite Books:
_____
_____
_____
_____

Favorite Place to Be:
_____
_____
_____
_____
_____
_____

My Friend's Wish:
_____
_____
_____
_____
_____
_____
_____

All About My Friend!

Name: _____

🧁 Birthday: _____   💎 Birthstone: _____

A Picture of My Friend:

Caption:
_____
_____
_____

Favorite Apps:
_____
_____
_____
_____
_____
_____
_____
_____
_____
_____
_____

Family:
_____
_____
_____
_____
_____

When They Grow Up They Want To Be:
_____
_____
_____
_____
_____

Favorite TV Shows:
_____
_____
_____
_____
_____

Other Favorites:
_____
_____
_____
_____
_____
_____

Favorite:

Color:_____
Number:_____
Candy:_____
Sport:_____
Team:_____
Store:_____
Food:_____
Vacation:_____
Animal:_____
Game:_____

Favorite Music:
_____
_____
_____
_____
_____
_____
_____

Hobbies: _____
_____
_____
_____

Favorite Books:
_____
_____
_____
_____

Favorite Place to Be:
_____
_____
_____
_____
_____
_____

My Friend's Wish:
_____
_____
_____
_____
_____

All About My Friend!

Name: _____

🧁 Birthday: _____   💎 Birthstone: _____

A Picture of My Friend:

Caption:
_____
_____
_____

Favorite Apps:
_____
_____
_____
_____
_____
_____
_____
_____
_____
_____
_____
_____

Family:
_____
_____
_____
_____
_____

When They Grow Up They Want To Be:
_____
_____
_____
_____
_____

Favorite TV Shows:
_____
_____
_____
_____
_____

Other Favorites:
_____
_____
_____
_____
_____
_____

Favorite:

Color:_____
Number:_____
Candy:_____
Sport:_____
Team:_____
Store:_____
Food:_____
Vacation:_____
Animal:_____
Game:_____

Favorite Music:
_____
_____
_____
_____
_____

Hobbies: _____
_____
_____
_____

Favorite Books:
_____
_____
_____
_____

Favorite Place to Be:
_____
_____
_____
_____
_____

My Friend's Wish:

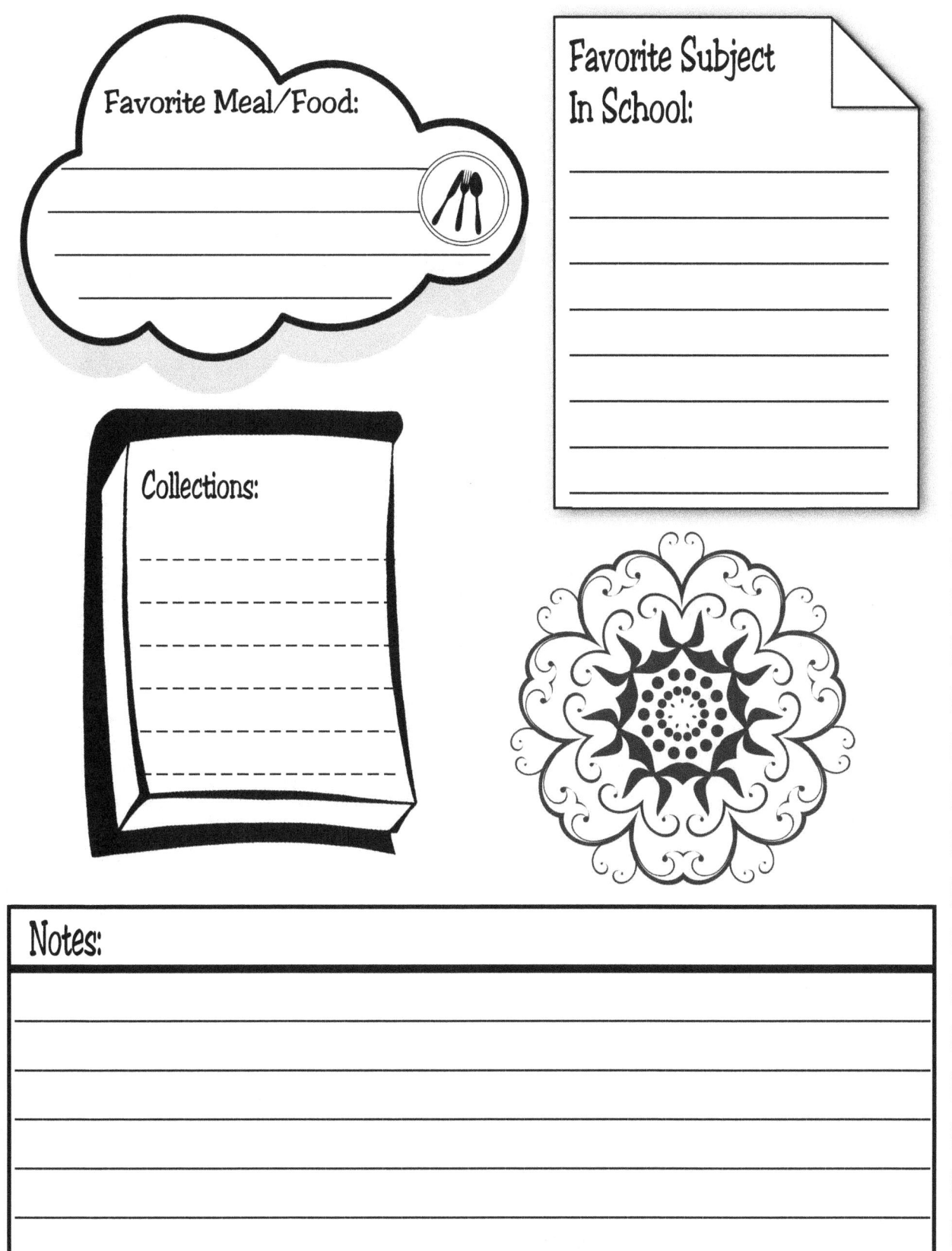

All About My Friend!

Name: _____

🧁 Birthday: _____   💎 Birthstone: _____

A Picture of My Friend:

Caption:
_____
_____
_____

Favorite Apps:
_____
_____
_____
_____
_____
_____
_____
_____
_____
_____
_____
_____

Family:
_____
_____
_____
_____
_____

When They Grow Up They Want To Be:
_____
_____
_____
_____
_____

Favorite TV Shows:
_____
_____
_____
_____

Other Favorites:
_____
_____
_____
_____
_____
_____

Favorite:

Color:_____
Number:_____
Candy:_____
Sport:_____
Team:_____
Store:_____
Food:_____
Vacation:_____
Animal:_____
Game:_____

Favorite Music:
_____
_____
_____
_____
_____

Hobbies: _____
_____
_____
_____

Favorite Books:
_____
_____
_____
_____

Favorite Place to Be:
_____
_____
_____
_____
_____

My Friend's Wish:
_____ _____
_____ _____
_____ _____
_____ _____
_____ _____
_____ _____

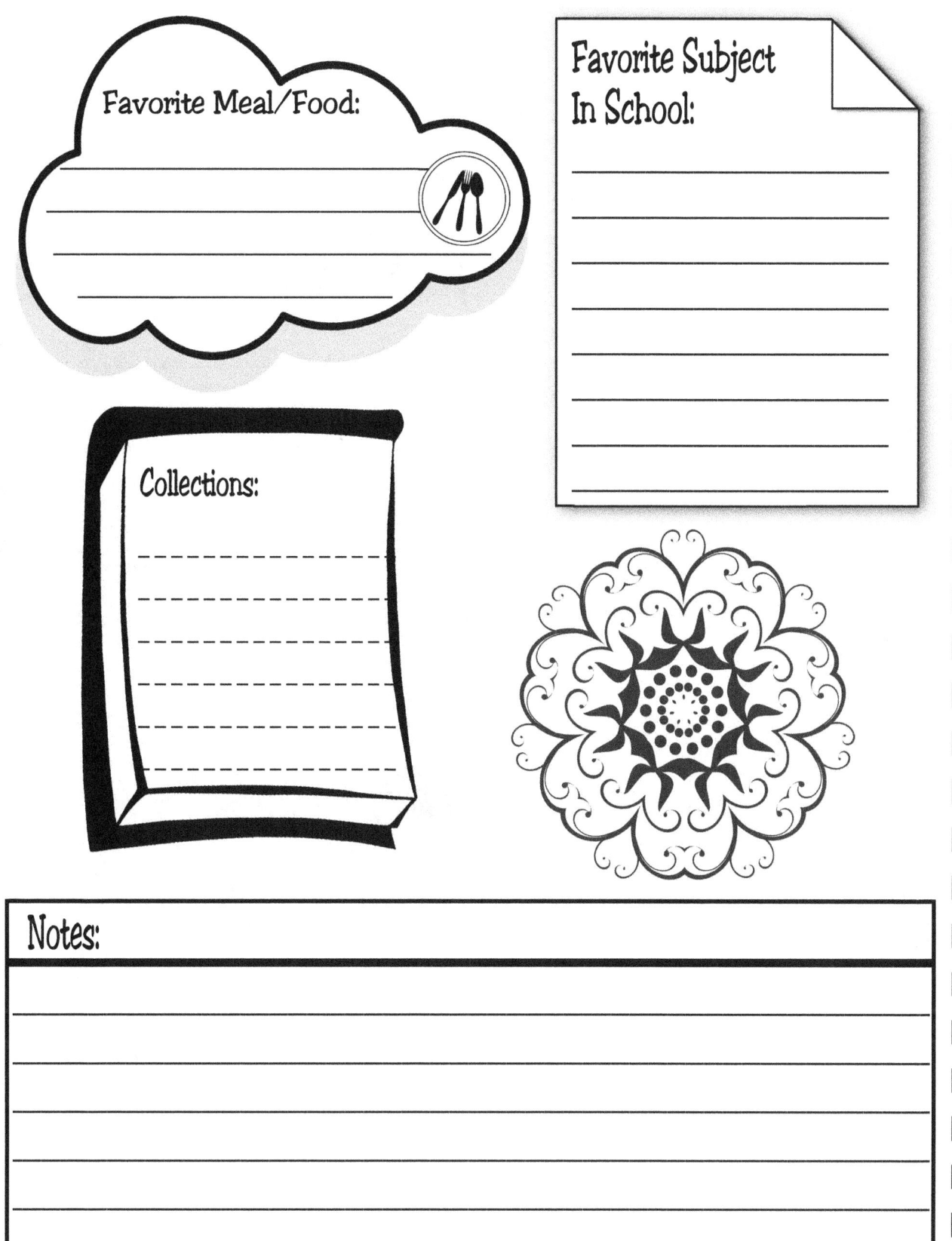

All About My Friend!

Name: _____

Birthday: _____   Birthstone: _____

A Picture of My Friend:

Caption:
_____
_____
_____

Favorite Apps:
_____
_____
_____
_____
_____
_____
_____
_____
_____
_____
_____
_____
_____

Family:
_____
_____
_____
_____
_____

When They Grow Up They Want To Be:
_____
_____
_____
_____
_____

Favorite TV Shows:
_____
_____
_____
_____

Other Favorites:
_____
_____
_____
_____
_____

Favorite:
Color: _____
Number: _____
Candy: _____
Sport: _____
Team: _____
Store: _____
Food: _____
Vacation: _____
Animal: _____
Game: _____

Favorite Music:
_____
_____
_____
_____
_____
_____

Hobbies: _____
_____
_____
_____

Favorite Books:
_____
_____
_____
_____

Favorite Place to Be:
_____
_____
_____
_____
_____
_____

My Friend's Wish:
_____   _____
_____   _____
_____   _____
_____   _____
_____   _____

Favorite Meal/Food:

Favorite Subject In School:

Collections:

Notes:

All About My Friend!

Name: _____

🧁 Birthday: _____   💎 Birthstone: _____

A Picture of My Friend:

Caption:
_____
_____
_____

Favorite Apps:
_____
_____
_____
_____
_____
_____
_____
_____
_____
_____
_____
_____

Family:
_____
_____
_____
_____
_____

When They Grow Up They Want To Be:
_____
_____
_____
_____
_____

Favorite TV Shows:
_____
_____
_____
_____
_____

Other Favorites:
_____
_____
_____
_____
_____
_____

Favorite:

Color:_____
Number:_____
Candy:_____
Sport:_____
Team:_____
Store:_____
Food:_____
Vacation:_____
Animal:_____
Game:_____

Favorite Music:
_____
_____
_____
_____
_____
_____
_____

Page 101

Hobbies: _____
_____
_____
_____

Favorite Books:
_____
_____
_____
_____

Favorite Place to Be:
_____
_____
_____
_____
_____
_____

My Friend's Wish:
_____
_____
_____
_____
_____

All About My Friend!

Name: _____

🧁 Birthday: _____ 💎 Birthstone: _____

A Picture of My Friend:

Caption:
_____
_____
_____

Favorite Apps:
_____
_____
_____
_____
_____
_____
_____
_____
_____
_____
_____
_____

Family:
_____
_____
_____
_____

When They Grow Up They Want To Be:
_____
_____
_____
_____

Favorite TV Shows:
_____
_____
_____
_____
_____

Other Favorites:
_____
_____
_____
_____
_____
_____

Favorite:
Color: _____
Number: _____
Candy: _____
Sport: _____
Team: _____
Store: _____
Food: _____
Vacation: _____
Animal: _____
Game: _____

Favorite Music:
_____
_____
_____
_____
_____
_____
_____

Hobbies: _____
_____
_____
_____

Favorite Books:
_____
_____
_____
_____

Favorite Place to Be:
_____
_____
_____
_____
_____

My Friend's Wish:
_____ _____
_____ _____
_____ _____
_____ _____
_____ _____

All About My Friend!

Name: _____

🧁 Birthday: _____ 💎 Birthstone: _____

A Picture of My Friend:

Caption: _____
_____
_____

Favorite Apps:
_____
_____
_____
_____
_____
_____
_____
_____
_____
_____

Family:
_____
_____
_____
_____

When They Grow Up They Want To Be:
_____
_____
_____
_____

Favorite TV Shows:

Other Favorites:

Favorite:

Color: _____
Number: _____
Candy: _____
Sport: _____
Team: _____
Store: _____
Food: _____
Vacation: _____
Animal: _____
Game: _____

Favorite Music:

Hobbies: _____
_____
_____
_____

Favorite Books:
_____
_____
_____
_____

Favorite Place to Be:
_____
_____
_____
_____
_____

My Friend's Wish:
_____
_____
_____
_____
_____

Favorite Meal/Food:

Favorite Subject In School:

Collections:

Notes:

All About My Friend!

Name: _____

🧁 Birthday: _____   💎 Birthstone: _____

A Picture of My Friend:

Caption:
_____
_____
_____

Favorite Apps:
_____
_____
_____
_____
_____
_____
_____
_____
_____
_____
_____

Family:
_____
_____
_____
_____

When They Grow Up They Want To Be:
_____
_____
_____
_____

Favorite TV Shows:

_____

_____

_____

_____

Other Favorites:

_____

_____

_____

_____

_____

Favorite:

Color: _____

Number: _____

Candy: _____

Sport: _____

Team: _____

Store: _____

Food: _____

Vacation: _____

Animal: _____

Game: _____

Favorite Music:

_____

_____

_____

_____

_____

_____

_____

Hobbies: _____
_____
_____
_____

Favorite Books:
_____
_____
_____
_____

Favorite Place to Be:
_____
_____
_____
_____
_____
_____

My Friend's Wish:
_____
_____
_____
_____
_____

All About My Friend!

Name: _____

🧁 Birthday: _____   💎 Birthstone: _____

A Picture of My Friend:

Caption:
_____
_____
_____

Favorite Apps:
_____
_____
_____
_____
_____
_____
_____
_____
_____
_____
_____
_____

Family:
_____
_____
_____
_____
_____

When They Grow Up They Want To Be:
_____
_____
_____
_____
_____

Favorite TV Shows:
_____
_____
_____
_____
_____

Other Favorites:
_____
_____
_____
_____
_____

Favorite:

Color: _____
Number: _____
Candy: _____
Sport: _____
Team: _____
Store: _____
Food: _____
Vacation: _____
Animal: _____
Game: _____

Favorite Music:
_____
_____
_____
_____
_____
_____
_____

Hobbies: _____
_____
_____
_____

Favorite Books:
_____
_____
_____
_____

Favorite Place to Be:
_____
_____
_____
_____
_____
_____

My Friend's Wish:
_____ _____
_____ _____
_____ _____
_____ _____
_____ _____

Favorite Meal/Food:

Favorite Subject In School:

Collections:

Notes:

All About My Friend!

Name: _____

Birthday: _____   Birthstone: _____

A Picture of My Friend:

Caption:
_____
_____
_____

Favorite Apps:
_____
_____
_____
_____
_____
_____
_____
_____
_____
_____
_____

Family:
_____
_____
_____
_____

When They Grow Up They Want To Be:
_____
_____
_____
_____

Favorite TV Shows:
_____
_____
_____
_____

Other Favorites:
_____
_____
_____
_____
_____
_____

Favorite:

Color: _____
Number: _____
Candy: _____
Sport: _____
Team: _____
Store: _____
Food: _____
Vacation: _____
Animal: _____
Game: _____

Favorite Music:
_____
_____
_____
_____
_____

Hobbies: _____
_____
_____
_____

Favorite Books:
_____
_____
_____
_____

Favorite Place to Be:
_____
_____
_____
_____
_____
_____

My Friend's Wish:

All About My Friend!

Name: _____

🧁 Birthday: _____ 💎 Birthstone: _____

A Picture of My Friend:

Caption:
_____
_____
_____

Favorite Apps:
_____
_____
_____
_____
_____
_____
_____
_____
_____
_____

Family:
_____
_____
_____
_____
_____

When They Grow Up They Want To Be:
_____
_____
_____
_____
_____

Favorite TV Shows:
_____
_____
_____
_____
_____

Other Favorites:
_____
_____
_____
_____
_____

Favorite:
Color:_____
Number:_____
Candy:_____
Sport:_____
Team:_____
Store:_____
Food:_____
Vacation:_____
Animal:_____
Game:_____

Favorite Music:
_____
_____
_____
_____
_____
_____
_____
_____

Hobbies: _____
_____
_____
_____

Favorite Books:
_____
_____
_____
_____

Favorite Place to Be:
_____
_____
_____
_____
_____
_____
_____

My Friend's Wish:
_____
_____
_____
_____
_____

All About My Friend!

Name: _____

🧁 Birthday: _____ 💎 Birthstone: _____

A Picture of My Friend:

Caption: _____
_____
_____

Favorite Apps:
_____
_____
_____
_____
_____
_____
_____
_____
_____
_____

Family:
_____
_____
_____
_____
_____

When They Grow Up They Want To Be:
_____
_____
_____
_____
_____

Favorite TV Shows:
_____
_____
_____
_____
_____

Other Favorites:
_____
_____
_____
_____
_____
_____

Favorite:

Color: _____
Number: _____
Candy: _____
Sport: _____
Team: _____
Store: _____
Food: _____
Vacation: _____
Animal: _____
Game: _____

Favorite Music:
_____
_____
_____
_____
_____
_____
_____

Hobbies: _____
_____
_____
_____

Favorite Books:
_____
_____
_____
_____

Favorite Place to Be:
_____
_____
_____
_____
_____
_____

My Friend's Wish:
_____
_____
_____
_____
_____
_____
_____
_____

All About My Friend!

Name: _____

🧁 Birthday: _____   💎 Birthstone: _____

A Picture of My Friend:

Caption:
_____
_____
_____

Favorite Apps:
_____
_____
_____
_____
_____
_____
_____
_____
_____
_____
_____

Family:
_____
_____
_____
_____
_____

When They Grow Up They Want To Be:
_____
_____
_____
_____
_____

Favorite TV Shows:
_____
_____
_____
_____

Other Favorites:
_____
_____
_____
_____
_____

Favorite:

Color: _____
Number: _____
Candy: _____
Sport: _____
Team: _____
Store: _____
Food: _____
Vacation: _____
Animal: _____
Game: _____

Favorite Music:
_____
_____
_____
_____
_____

Hobbies: _____
_____
_____
_____

Favorite Books:
_____
_____
_____
_____

Favorite Place to Be:
_____
_____
_____
_____
_____
_____

My Friend's Wish:
_____
_____
_____
_____
_____
_____

Favorite Meal/Food:

Favorite Subject In School:

Collections:

Notes:

All About My Friend!

Name: _____

🧁 Birthday: _____ 💎 Birthstone: _____

A Picture of My Friend:

Caption:
_____
_____
_____

Favorite Apps:
_____
_____
_____
_____
_____
_____
_____
_____
_____
_____

Family:
_____
_____
_____
_____
_____

When They Grow Up They Want To Be:
_____
_____
_____
_____
_____

Favorite TV Shows:
_____
_____
_____
_____
_____

Other Favorites:
_____
_____
_____
_____
_____
_____

Favorite:

Color: _____
Number: _____
Candy: _____
Sport: _____
Team: _____
Store: _____
Food: _____
Vacation: _____
Animal: _____
Game: _____

Favorite Music:
_____
_____
_____
_____
_____
_____
_____
_____

Hobbies: _____
_____
_____
_____

Favorite Books:
_____
_____
_____
_____

Favorite Place to Be:
_____
_____
_____
_____
_____
_____
_____

My Friend's Wish:

All About My Friend!

Name: _____

Birthday: _____   Birthstone: _____

A Picture of My Friend:

Caption:
_____
_____
_____

Favorite Apps:
_____
_____
_____
_____
_____
_____
_____
_____
_____
_____
_____
_____

Family:
_____
_____
_____
_____
_____

When They Grow Up They Want To Be:
_____
_____
_____
_____
_____

Favorite TV Shows:
_____
_____
_____
_____
_____

Other Favorites:
_____
_____
_____
_____
_____
_____

Favorite:

Color: _____
Number: _____
Candy: _____
Sport: _____
Team: _____
Store: _____
Food: _____
Vacation: _____
Animal: _____
Game: _____

Favorite Music:
_____
_____
_____
_____
_____
_____

Hobbies: _____
_____
_____
_____

Favorite Books:
_____
_____
_____
_____

Favorite Place to Be:
_____
_____
_____
_____
_____

My Friend's Wish:
_____
_____
_____
_____
_____

All About My Friend!

Name: _____

🧁 Birthday: _____ 💎 Birthstone: _____

A Picture of My Friend:

Caption:
_____
_____
_____

Favorite Apps:
_____
_____
_____
_____
_____
_____
_____
_____
_____
_____
_____

Family:
_____
_____
_____
_____

When They Grow Up They Want To Be:
_____
_____
_____
_____

Favorite TV Shows:

_____
_____
_____
_____
_____

Other Favorites:

_____
_____
_____
_____
_____
_____

Favorite:

Color:_____
Number:_____
Candy:_____
Sport:_____
Team:_____
Store:_____
Food:_____
Vacation:_____
Animal:_____
Game:_____

Favorite Music:

_____
_____
_____
_____
_____

Hobbies: _____
_____
_____
_____

Favorite Books:
_____
_____
_____
_____

Favorite Place to Be:
_____
_____
_____
_____
_____
_____
_____

My Friend's Wish:
_____ _____
_____ _____
_____ _____
_____ _____
_____ _____

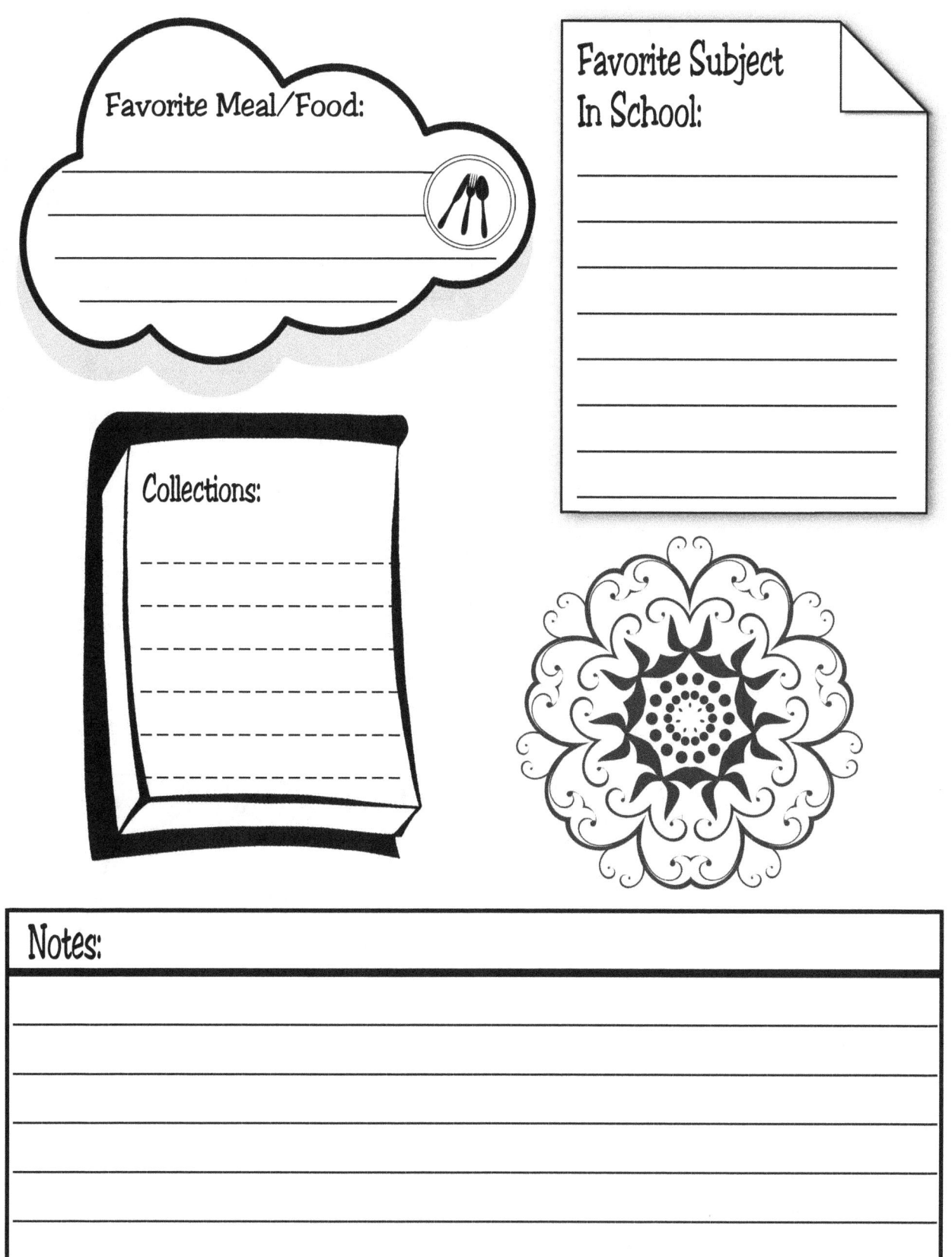

All About My Friend!

Name: _____

🧁 **Birthday:** _____ 💎 **Birthstone:** _____

A Picture of My Friend:

[ ]

Caption:
_____
_____
_____

Favorite Apps:
_____
_____
_____
_____
_____
_____
_____
_____
_____
_____
_____

Family:
_____
_____
_____
_____

When They Grow Up They Want To Be:
_____
_____
_____
_____

Favorite TV Shows:
_____
_____
_____
_____
_____

Other Favorites:
_____
_____
_____
_____
_____
_____

Favorite:

Color: _____
Number: _____
Candy: _____
Sport: _____
Team: _____
Store: _____
Food: _____
Vacation: _____
Animal: _____
Game: _____

Favorite Music:
_____
_____
_____
_____
_____
_____
_____

Hobbies: _____
_____
_____
_____

Favorite Books:
_____
_____
_____
_____

Favorite Place to Be:
_____
_____
_____
_____
_____
_____

My Friend's Wish:
_____
_____
_____
_____

All About My Friend!

Name: _____

🧁 Birthday: _____ 💎 Birthstone: _____

A Picture of My Friend:

Caption:
_____
_____
_____

Favorite Apps:
_____
_____
_____
_____
_____
_____
_____
_____
_____
_____
_____

Family:
_____
_____
_____
_____
_____

When They Grow Up They Want To Be:
_____
_____
_____
_____
_____

Favorite TV Shows:
_____
_____
_____
_____
_____

Other Favorites:
_____
_____
_____
_____
_____

Favorite:

Color:_____
Number:_____
Candy:_____
Sport:_____
Team:_____
Store:_____
Food:_____
Vacation:_____
Animal:_____
Game:_____

Favorite Music:
_____
_____
_____
_____
_____
_____

Hobbies: _____
_____
_____
_____

Favorite Books:
_____
_____
_____
_____

Favorite Place to Be:
_____
_____
_____
_____
_____

My Friend's Wish:
_____ _____
_____ _____
_____ _____
_____ _____
_____ _____

Autographs

Autographs

A Humble Request,

If you find this handbook helpful, please consider leaving an honest review online.

A sentence or two is fine for your review.

You can find all my books on my Amazon author page:
www.amazon.com/author/dianalynn

Thank you,

Diana Lynn

ISBN: 978-1-947594-91-3
Published by D&D Graphics in 2017
First edition; First printing

Design, and writing Copyright © 2017 Diana Lynn
website: dianalynnwrites.com